SUPER SHARKS

CONTENTS

what is a shark?	2
baby sharks	4
clever camouflage	6
great white shark	8
hammerhead shark	10
tiger shark	12
bull shark	14
whale shark	16
weird and wonderful	18
megalodon	20
sharks in danger	22
glossary	24

WHAT IS A SHARK?

Sharks are a group of fish that can be found all over the world in oceans and even some rivers! With over 450 different types, they range from the tiny dwarf lantern shark to the enormous whale shark!

whale shark

PARTS OF A SHARK

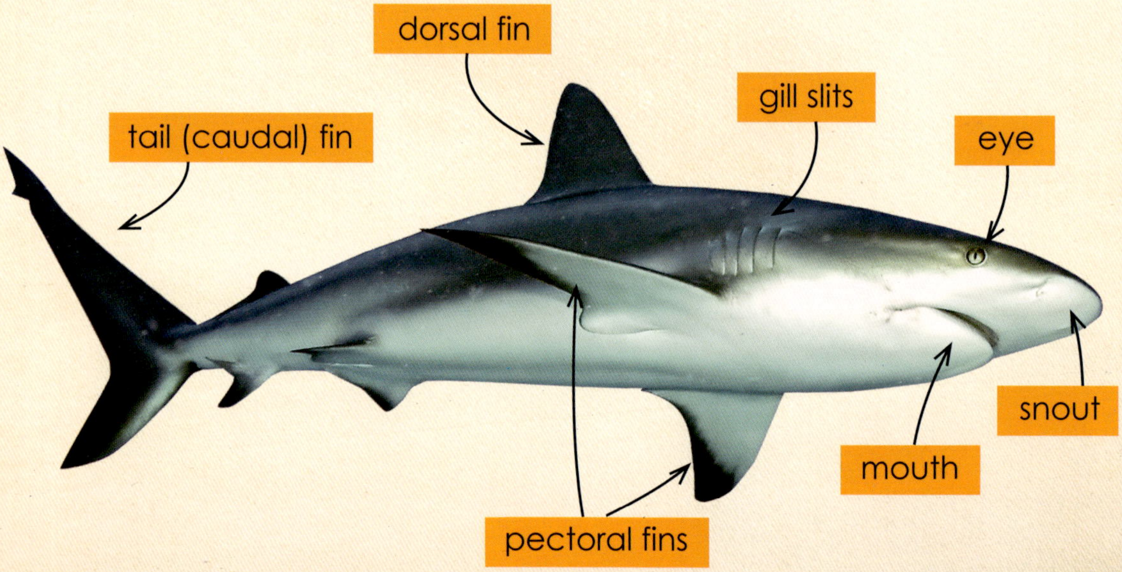

- dorsal fin
- tail (caudal) fin
- gill slits
- eye
- snout
- mouth
- pectoral fins

reef shark

Sixth sense

Sharks have senses like we do. However, they also have an extra sense. Special organs allow them to sense the electrical impulses of their prey.

BABY SHARKS

lemon shark pup

Sharks give birth in lots of different ways. Most sharks give birth to live young and some lay eggs. Baby sharks are known as pups.

WHAT DO WE KNOW?

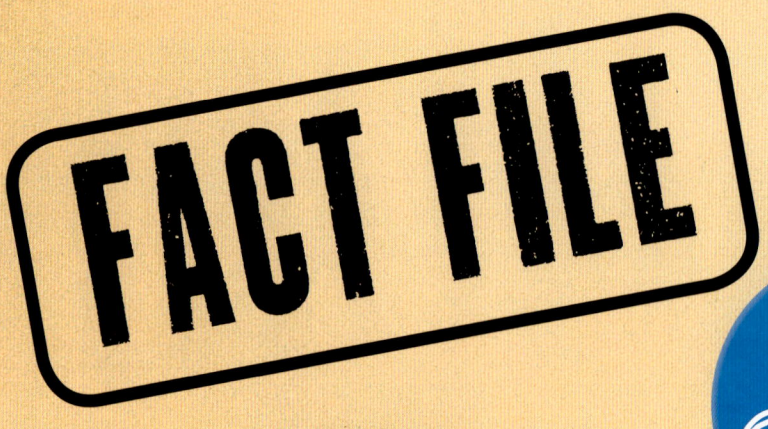

FACT FILE

MORE FIN-TASTIC FACTS!

Fun fact!
A shark's egg case is also known as a mermaid's purse. When empty, they often wash up on beaches for people to find!

Port Jackson shark

CLEVER CAMOUFLAGE

tasselled wobbegong shark

Some sharks have markings that blend in with their surroundings. This helps them to attack their prey by surprise or hide from predators.

SPOT THE SHARK!

Some species of shark can glow in the dark. This makes them harder to spot against the faint glow of sunlight.

swell shark

7

GREAT WHITE SHARK

Great white sharks are the largest predatory shark in the oceans. They have all the tools they need to be effective hunters.

WHAT DO WE KNOW?

FOR SHARK SUPER-FANS ONLY!

Speedy hunters
Great white sharks often attack fast-moving prey from below by launching themselves out of the water. This is called breaching.

HAMMERHEAD SHARK

great hammerhead shark

This family of sharks have unusual-shaped heads that look like hammers.

WHAT DO WE KNOW?

FACT FILE

FOR SHARK SUPER-FANS ONLY!

Super sight

A hammerhead shark has eyes on either side of its head. This gives it super-sight because it can see 360° at all times!

great hammerhead shark

Fun fact!
There are eight species of hammerhead shark. The great hammerhead is the largest!

great hammerhead shark

TIGER SHARK

These super scavengers are famous for eating almost anything, even car license plates and tires!

WHAT DO WE KNOW?

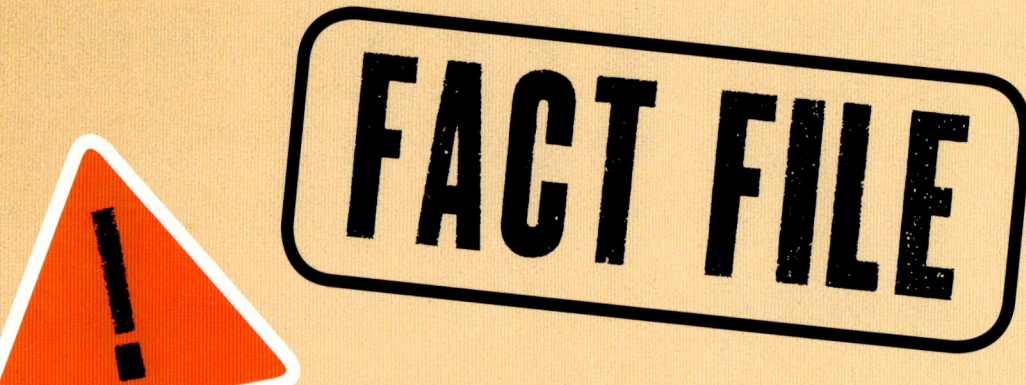

FACT FILE

SCARY SHARK FACTS INSIDE

Fun fact!
Tiger sharks get their name from the stripes on their bodies! The stripes are dark when they are young, but paler in adults.

BULL SHARK

Similar to bulls, these sharks can be aggressive, are thickly built, and have been known to head-butt their prey!

WHAT DO WE KNOW?

FACT FILE

FOR SHARK SUPER-FANS ONLY!

Fun fact!
Most sharks need to live in salt water. However, bull sharks can retain salt in their bodies, so they are able to live in freshwater lakes and rivers.

The Amazon River

WHALE SHARK

The whale shark is the largest fish in the sea. At up to 46 ft (14 m), this shark can be as long as a school bus!

WHAT DO WE KNOW?

FACT FILE

SHARK SCIENTISTS ONLY!

Fun fact!
Just like with human fingerprints, the spotted patterns on whale sharks' skin are unique. This means each whale shark has a different pattern!

WEIRD AND WONDERFUL

There are many shapes and sizes of sharks that range from the wonderful to the bizarre. Some have long tails, some are fast, some are slow, and one can even walk!

RECORD BREAKERS

Farthest

blue shark

Fastest

shortfin mako shark

Oldest

Greenland shark

Longest tail

thresher shark

A CLOSER LOOK

epaulette shark

The epaulette shark can survive for long periods without oxygen, which allows it to walk across the coral reef on its fins!

WHAT DO WE KNOW?

FOR SHARK SPECIALISTS ONLY!

MEGALODON

artist's impression of megalodon

This powerful shark became extinct about 2 million years ago. Scientists think it was the biggest shark that has ever lived.

WHAT DO WE KNOW?

FACT FILE

FOSSIL HUNTERS ONLY!

life-size crocodile tooth

life-size great white tooth

life-size dog tooth

What did it eat?
It probably ate large, prehistoric prey such as whales, big fish, dolphins, and other sharks.

SHARKS IN DANGER

Some sharks are endangered, which means they are at risk of dying out completely. They are being overfished for food or caught by people for sport.

WHAT ARE THE THREATS?

Caribbean reef shark